To Lola

Dream big

x x x

I Can't Not Never

Not Be Very Tall

My name is Jessica and here's the thing

I can shout and scream and run and sing

But my body won't grow much at all

I can't not never not be very tall.

I can hop and bounce and scream and shout

And run around with my hair flying out

I can dance and sing and ride and hide

But I can't climb the steps to the slide.

I can draw and write with a pencil or a pen

I draw the numbers all the way to ten

I like to paint with purple and pink

But I can't reach to wash in the sink

I struggle sometimes when climbing the stairs

Watching other children taking them in pairs

I huff as others run and leap

Finding it easy where I find it steep.

I'm the last to be picked for any game, sport or match

I'm always the smallest kid in any batch

The bullies see me as an easy target

I'm tougher than I look, and don't you forget it.

I have to climb to sit on a chair

But I will find my own way there

I need a step to reach the loo

But remember, so did all of you.

I hold a pen, maybe not the same way you do

But I write my name and I draw things too

I know my numbers, colours and shapes

And play superheroes with my capes

I can run, jump, skip and hop

I can start, go, slow and stop

I can roll, hide, crawl and seek

I can nosey, look, cheat and peak

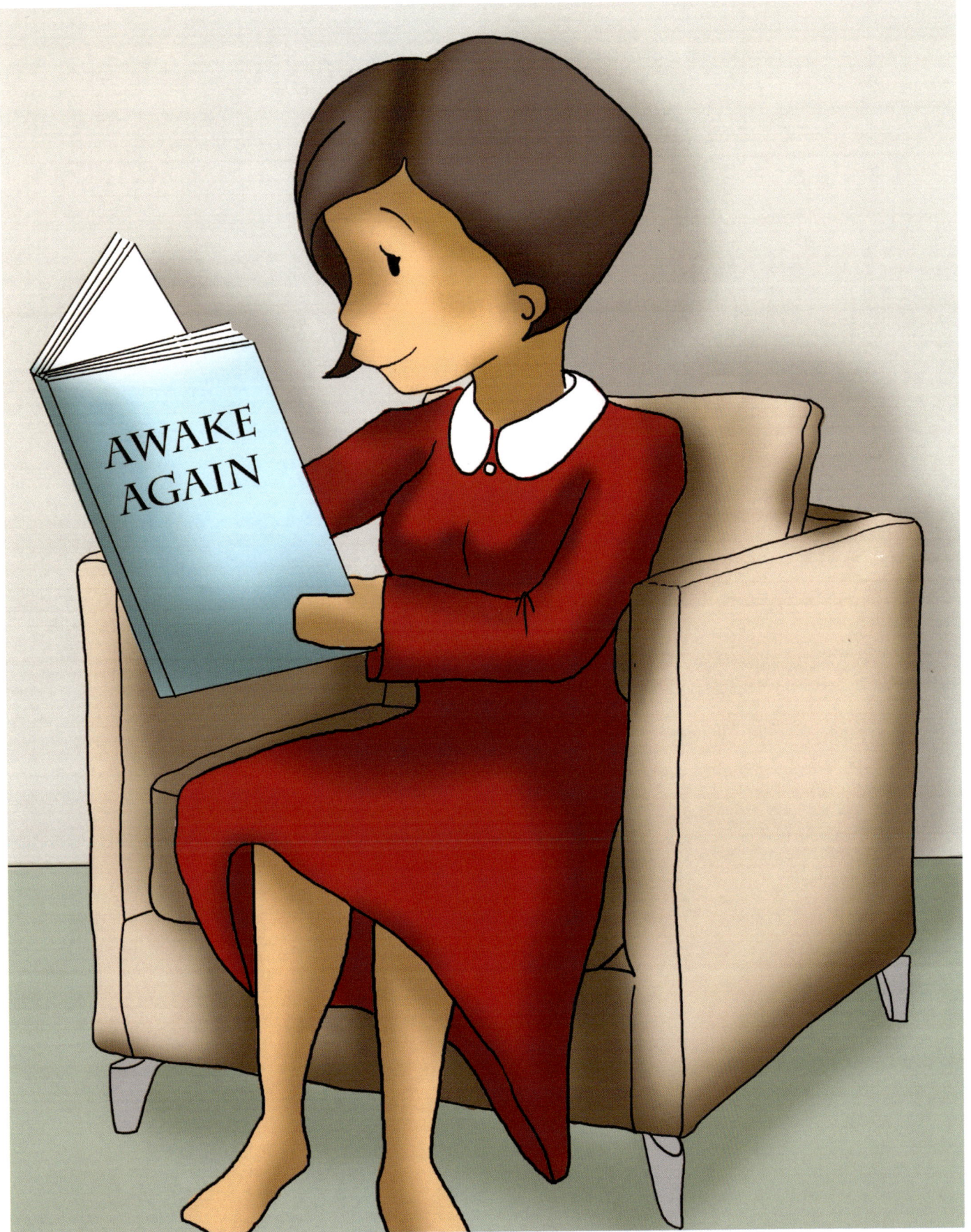

I can crawl through a pipe, I'm a secret agent

I can get information from a spy who's resistant

I can play pretend from heroes to tea parties

I can even open my own pack of sweeties.

If you think I need help, just sit back and watch

I can always ask if it turns out a botch

I'll forever be helpless if I never try

but I know you'll be there, when I can't get by

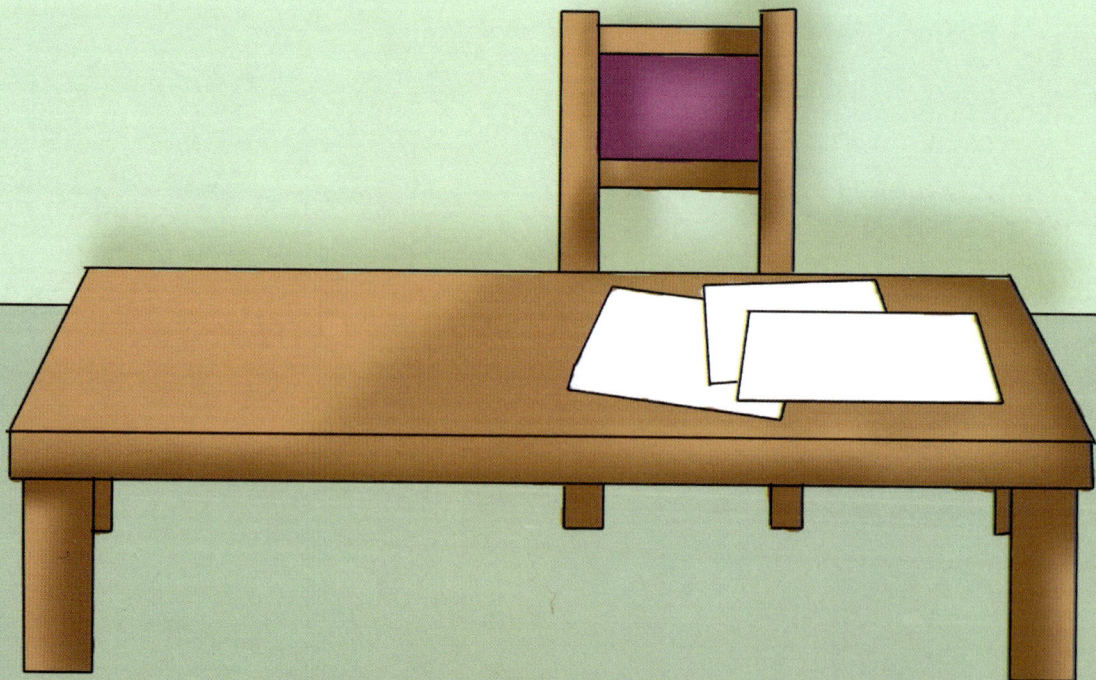

My name is Jessica and I am small

I can't not never not be very tall

But being small is not so bad

Actually, I think it's really fab.

Jessica was born with a rare medical condition
known as Achondroplasia, Dwarfism.
She will always be smaller than most others
and will always need a little extra help with things.
But she needs to be given the chance
to try things the same as every other person does.
It's nice when others want to help.
But sometimes it's nicer when others help
by letting her do it herself.
All you need to remember is that
if she really needs help with something
she can always ask.

Made in the USA
Charleston, SC
07 September 2014